Turn Around Trauma:

How to Live Your Best Life After Adversity

Dr. Richard K. Nongard

Turn Around Trauma: How to Live Your Best Life After Adversity by Dr. Richard K. Nongard

Copyright © 2019 by Dr. Richard K. Nongard

All Rights Reserved.

No part of this publication may be reproduced, distributed, or transmitted in any form or by any means, including photocopying, recording, or other electronic or mechanical methods, without the prior written permission from the author, except in the case of brief quotations embodied in critical reviews and certain other non-commercial uses permitted by copyright law.

The stories in this book are fictional representations of typical cases Dr. Nongard has worked with. Names, characters, places and incidents are products of the author's imagination or are used fictitiously. Any resemblance to actual events, locales, or persons living or dead is entirely coincidental.

First Printing: November 20193

ISBN-13: 9781703092776

Dr. Richard K. Nongard

15560 N. Frank L. Wright Blvd. B4-118

Scottsdale, AZ 85260

(702) 418-3332

TurnAroundTrauma.com | NongardBooks.com

Dr. Nongard is available to be a speaker at your event and speaks on a variety of topics.

Table of Contents

About Dr. Richard K. Nongard: 5
CHAPTER ONE: Our Past Creates our Present 7
CHAPTER TWO: How Trauma Traps Us 21
CHAPTER THREE: Freedom and Love......................31
CHAPTER FOUR: Acceptance, Distancing, Defusion, Resilience 41
CHAPTER FIVE: What it was like, what happened and what it's like now 55
CHAPTER SIX: Making Mindfulness Real.................65
CHAPTER SEVEN: Bilateral stimulation....................77
CHAPTER EIGHT: Security and Significance.............83
CHAPTER NINE: Getting Additional Help 89
CHAPTER TEN: Oogway's gift..................................95

About Dr. Richard K. Nongard:

Dr. Richard K. Nongard is a Licensed Marriage and Family Therapist, and the author of numerous books on counseling, hypnotherapy, mindfulness, and leadership. Dr. Nongard is a frequent conference and keynote speaker for community organizations, mental health groups, and businesses.

His most recent notable accomplishment was sharing his story, and how mindfulness can transform your life, at TEDx Oklahoma City in April of 2019.

Dr. Nongard has completed his Doctorate in Transformational Leadership with a concentration in Cultural Transformation through Bakke Graduate University. BGU is a nationally accredited university, accredited by an accreditor which is recognized by both the United States Department of Education (USDOE) and the Council for Higher Education Accreditation (CHEA). He holds a masters degree in counseling from Liberty University (Class of 1990).

Dr. Richard K. Nongard

Richard is an innovative leader in the field of psychotherapy and Mindfulness, and over the last 25+ years he has trained thousands of professionals including ministers, medical doctors, psychologists, social workers, family therapists, hypnotherapists and professional counselors in ways to do a better job serving their clients.

He is the author of many textbooks and resources. Recent titles include:

The Step-Spouse: How to Stay Sane when Their Ex is Driving you Crazy

Real-Hope: How Hope Drives Positive Actions that Lead to Business, Leadership and Real-World Victory

Viral Leadership: Seize the Power of Now to Create Lasting Transformation in Business

CHAPTER ONE:

Our Past Creates our Present

Our past creates our present. It brings us to exactly where we are today. But the paradox of the past is that even though it brought us to where we are, the past does not determine the future.

By understanding our past, we can predict the future with great accuracy. The amazing thing is that each one of us can break the predictive cycles of the past and create a new manor of living. We can do it now, we can do it at any time, and we can do it even against all odds.

This means that if your past has created a present moment that is anxious, depressing, painful, angry or self-defeating, it is possible to break this state and step into abundance, self-control, better relationships, improved finances, and even happiness or joy.

This is an extravagant promise but dramatic changes in predictive life trajectories occur every day. The academic research in psychology and other fields show it. I am a licensed psychotherapist, and some of my clients create a breakthrough and break free of their past

– even the excruciatingly traumatic pasts that brought them to my office in the first place. I am also a survivor, breaking a multi-generational history of family addiction. My father died from his addiction at 42. As a child, I never saw him breathe a sober breath. At the time of this writing I am 54. I have not had a drink in 31 years. My adult children have never seen me drunk.

What is your story? What were your experiences? What brought you to the point where you are reading this book today? Many of my clients feel they are chained to their past; here are some of their stories…

Bob's Story

A gentleman named Bob was a client I saw for treatment of a life-long eating disorder. He was 200 pounds overweight and had been binging and purging for decades. Eating disorders are almost always associated with younger women. Nobody suspected Bob was consumed day and night with his battle with Bulimia. His family didn't know, his healthcare providers never screened for it, and society never told Bob that, "Yes, middle-aged male attorneys can have an eating disorder too." He knew something was wrong but didn't know what.

Bob ended up in my office when a bariatric surgeon ruled him out as a candidate for surgery because of the heart problems he had developed as a result of his condition. Bob just thought he was fat. But he met every diagnostic criterion for an eating disorder, and up to this point nobody had noticed. All he knew was that he was in pain. Food brought him happiness, and food made him hate himself. Bob binged, and Bob purged. Bob was killing himself.

A simple assessment, known as the Assessment of Adverse Childhood Experiences, revealed that Bob was a survivor of multiple childhood traumas. Anyone with basic Freudian assessment skills could see that Bob had internalized his rage, his grief, his fear, and his pain and created a self-destructive set of coping skills. I'll leave it to the Freudians to guess why an eating disorder developed, but we do know that his pain, both physical and emotional, brought him to where he was the first time he walked into my office. His depression had long since turned to despair, and I still remember how profoundly hopeless he believed himself to be.

Bobs father was an alcoholic. His father raged at his mother, cheated on his mother, and hit his mother. Bob's parents divorced when he was 10 and his mother remarried another man who mirrored many of the same traits. Bob found comfort as a teen on one thing, his religion and his role as an altar boy. Are you guessing what came next? Yes, he was a victim of childhood sexual abuse.

How he had graduated from law school and started a successful practice and maintained a reasonably happy marriage for 20+ years is a story of resilience. It is an amazing story of strength and hope, but Bob didn't see it that way and now his eating disorder was killing him.

Terry's Story

Terry felt like she was out of control. She knew her own behavior was ruining her marriage, making her children despise her and her anxiety was now rising to a level where she was almost trapped in her home. She would wake up after a few hours of fretful sleep and immediately dread the day. Her knee-jerk reaction to everybody around her was a pattern her husband had long grown tired of. She started fights clearly believing that, by being proactive to address any failed expectations of others, she would have the upper hand. She knew exactly why nobody wanted to be around her. Her friends had avoided her, even her own mother seemed to avoid her. She knew, because she didn't want to be around herself either. She was depressed, ineffective and tired.

Terry had talents. She was a magnificent singer, she did work as a backup studio vocalist on numerous commercial music tracks, some that had made it bigtime, and she hung out with the rich and famous. Outwardly she was a success, but inside her own home, and certainly in her own spirit, she was an emotional, and behavioral wreck.

Her history? Family addiction. Her father was incarcerated for stealing copper wire during the economic hardships of the late 1970's and although her current marriage had lasted 15 years, she had been married twice before in whirlwind relationships that each lasted less than a year. She often laid in bed and just wondered what it would be like to have a "normal life" and sometimes wondering if it were still possible for her.

These examples may seem extreme, but they are actually common examples of how adverse childhood traumas affect us long after our childhood is over. Adverse Childhood Experiences have proven to be widespread across every demographic and income group in America. And while both of these examples deal primarily with emotions and behaviors, adverse childhood experiences are also predictors of physical wellbeing long after the trauma has taken place. Heart disease, stroke, cancer, depression, addiction, diabetes and many other chronic health conditions are observed at exponential rates among those who have been traumatized as children.

Do you often feel that your past has trapped you into a vicious cycle of pain and self-inflicted misery? Do you find that when you try to break free, that past seems to rope you back in?

This book is for people who have experienced psychological trauma and want to develop resiliency and establish a sense of both security and significance. A traumatic event is defined as one in which you perceive a threat to your life, bodily integrity, or sanity. Many people who have experienced trauma feel a lack of security in present situations. They often feel consumed with fear and anxiety as a result of this trauma and are unsure of how to handle present day situations. It can also create physical illness. It can create emotional stress. Trauma survivors have self-doubt, they relive past traumas in new situations, and find life difficult.

Have you experienced traumatic events? Some people have had more than others and in varying degrees of severity. It is important to note, life is not a competitive misery contest and even one significant traumatic event can have lifelong ramifications. The number of traumas a person has experienced will not necessarily correlate to the level of difficulties they have. The effects can be emotional, behavioral, and manifest in our relationships.

Ten common adverse childhood experiences include:

- Physical abuse
- Sexual abuse
- Emotional abuse
- Physical neglect
- Emotional neglect
- Exposure to domestic violence
- Household substance abuse
- Household mental illness
- Parental separation or divorce
- Incarcerated household member

Any of these can have significant traumatic experiences alongside them. Other frequent traumas that <u>both</u> adults and children can experience include:

- Accidents
- Bullying/Cyberbullying

- Sexual Assault
- Violent crime
- War/terrorism
- Divorce
- Illness
- Death of a family member
- Economic insecurity
- Natural disaster
- Intimate Partner Violence
- Sexual exploitation

This is by no means an exhaustive list. The possibilities of traumatic experience are unlimited, but the types of traumas on this list are often reported, and often the source of significant emotional distress. That distress is not short-lived. The effects can endure at one level or another throughout the lifespan.

As a therapist, I often meet people who are highly traumatized from a multiplicity of traumas, but do not recognize the severity of either their experience or the depth of pain these wounds have created. They do not make a connection between the events of the past, and the problems they have today. Some people know they have had trauma but believe they have no lasting effects of their previous traumas, but as an outside observer, I clearly see the connection. These problems might include things like:

- Chronic anxiety and stress
- Relationship instability
- Sexual dysfunction
- Work and vocational problems
- Parenting difficulties
- Social difficulties
- Financial trouble
- Anger, anxiety, and depression.

Ask yourself these questions:

- Do you have ongoing health issues and chronic conditions that require medical treatment?
- Are you overweight?
- Do you drink or use drugs to make you feel better?
- Do you have mood swings, anger, anxiety, or depression frequently?
- Are you startled easily?
- Do you have insomnia or sleep difficulties that affect your wellbeing?
- Do you feel a sense of disconnect from other people, a lack of empathy, or feel that people don't understand you?
- Do you have difficulty concentrating, learning, or following directions?
- Do you withdraw from others?

- Are you dissatisfied with intimacy, sex and love?
- Do you feel that life is chaotic and that things are unstable?
- Do you question your purpose, value, or self-worth?
- Are you often feeling guilt or shame?

Any affirmative answers may mean that you have been affected by previous life traumas and will benefit from the solutions in this book.

Are you ready to step into a new chapter of life and put the effects of previous life traumas to rest and start experiencing a new manor of living? Even if you think it is impossible to feel interest and joy in everyday life, would you like to experience this joy and find life interesting if you could?

Let me ask you a few more questions…

What would it be like for you to be able to think about your traumatic past and feel totally free from any negative emotions attached to it?

What would it be like to have a truly healthy relationship with others, even those who might have hurt you?

What would it be like to know that although everyone has anxiety from time to time, you don't have to suffer from it?

What would it be like to love yourself? Truly love yourself? And be able to love other people?

This book is packed with solutions you can start

using today that are based on doable principles of making lasting change. The result will bring a new sense of peace, a sense of security and a feeling of accomplishment. The best part? You will be able to see not only a clear path to changing the impact of trauma, but you will even be able to see how your experiences can benefit others.

You can change a multi-generational pattern of trauma and help your children live a different life than you have lived. You will be able to find healthy love and create lasting relationships. You will be able to heal your wounds, both emotional and physical and step into health each and every day.

Not all our traumas come from childhood. Adulthood can have its own set of traumas. Perhaps your childhood home was idyllic, but something happened long after childhood was over. Were you in an abusive relationship? It's probably taking its toll on your current relationship. Did you make a million and then lose it, struggling ever since that time to have another opportunity to rise from the ashes? Were you the victim of a crime, an accident, or some other unpredictable trauma?

Were you shunned as an adult because the religious community (and your parents) responded with hate to your sexuality, your questioning of their dogma, or a behavior they saw as an unforgivable transgression? I had a friend, Kris, who had grown up with a mentally ill mother who was a member of a Fundamentalist Church. She was taken out of school to pass out tracts on the side of the street. The religion taught the end of the Earth was near, and that anyone who did not follow the teachings were putting their eternity into jeopardy. But, she liked music. She liked school. She wanted to read schoolbooks and not pass out tracts. She was the black sheep of the family. When she announced she was a lesbian at the age of 23, her family and friends cut her from their lives.

Abuse and neglect can take many forms. Trauma can take many forms. In 1990, I was on an Eastern Airline flight from Atlanta to Roanoke. I can't really recall all the details, but it was a traumatic flight. It was on a regional turbo-prop, It started with storms and then turbulence, and then people screaming and praying and the pilot telling us to brace upon landing.

Fortunately, it did not result in a crash, but it was more severe than an emergency landing. I have referred to it since this day as a "belly-flop" landing. We exited the plane down the fold-our stairs, jelly-legged from our fear, and onto the rain-soaked tarmac. I vowed I would never get on a plane again.

I have struggled with anxiety all my life. The root of this anxiety was probably an unpredictable childhood with an alcoholic father, a confusing blended-family, and the eventual death of my father when I was a teen. But this flight turned my fear of flying into a phobia. Eleven years later, in 2001, I had a friend who was both a pilot and psychologist help me over my fear of flying. He took me up in his plane on a beautiful August afternoon. He taught me how a plane works, he taught me a little about how ot fly and even let me have the controls for a moment. He helped me with my anxiety, assuring me that its safer to fly than to drive and that I could use the same techniques to control anxiety that I teach my therapy clients, to overcome my fear of flying.

He told me that now that I was "over" my fear of flying, I should buy a ticket on Southwest Airlines to ratify the change, and begin my new chapter of life without a fear of flying. I was so excited when I went home, I bought a ticket. My ticket was scheduled for the days immediately following September 11, 2001. The flight that I had purchased in the days following was grounded. It never took off. All flights were grounded nationwide for days. It wasn't until 2003, almost two years later, that I finally took that flight.

It is ironic, but I am actually writing this book from a turbulent plane with the pilot announcing that the seatbelt sign will be staying on while flying from Las Vegas, where I live, to Chicago where I am speaking about hypnotherapy to help people overcome their fear of flying!

Eventually, my client Bob not only lost enough weight to stay healthy and broke the pattern of his eating-disorder. Terry eventually stopped her self-destructive behavior and began repairing her relationship with her family. Kris never did gain her family of origin back, but became a leader in a new community where she was able to help others based on her experience and found peace in a non-fear based religion. I have flown over a million miles since I overcame my fear of flying, a testament to the fact that we can overcome the traumas we experience no matter how difficult they are.

Whatever happened to you, both the major traumas like Adverse Childhood Experiences (ACEs) or the complications in adulthood that were both major traumas and little traumas, did bring you to the point where you are right now. Many people do get trapped by their traumas and stay stuck. They never move into a pattern where the cycles are broken. But many others are, each and every day, getting better and better in each and every way.

Do you want to be a part of this group? The group that breaks the cycle of pain and despair, the part of the group that gets on the horse again after falling off the first time (or second, third, fourth…)? Are you ready for improved relationships, better self-control and a feeling of both security and significance?

If so, get ready to apply the learnings in this book. When you are finished with this book, you will have numerus strategies based both on the research into trauma recovery, my experiences working with clients in professional therapy, and yes, even ideas I have adapted in my own life to break the patterns of my own ACEs. (To learn more about my personal journey in an alcoholic family system, see my TEDx Oklahoma City talk at www.TurnAroundTrauma.com)

CHAPTER TWO:

How Trauma Traps Us

One of my favorite TED talks is by pediatrician Nadine Burke Harris. She is also the first surgeon general appointed by the State of California. She tells us that trauma activates the hypothalamic-pituitary-adrenal axis system. This axis is designed to activate the flight or fight response and protect us. In her talk, she discusses what it would be like to run into a bear in the forest. She explains, "Your hypothalamus sends a signal to your pituitary who then sends a signal to the adrenal glad that says: release stress hormones, adrenaline and cortisol!"

The result of seeing this bear is that your eyes dilate and your airways open and you are now ready to fight this bear or run from it. She points out the obvious: "This is wonderful if you are in a forest and there's a bear." But then she asks a really pointed question, directly related to Adverse Childhood Experiences (ACEs): "But what happens when the bear comes home every night, and this system is activated over and over again, and it goes from being adaptive or life-saving to maladaptive or health damaging." The result of activating this response over and over in the life of a child are not only psychological wounds, but literal physical changes in the structure of the brain and bodies of these children.

In a TEDx talk I did in Oklahoma City, titled *Mindfulness: How to Transform Your Life,* I share how evolutionary biology created stress responses over millions of years to help us deal, as a species, with cataclysmic disaster, famine, harsh conditions, family death. It also developed the skill of being able to quickly scan our mental hard drive of previous experiences, to help us make a reasonable prediction about the present. In its simplest form, it explains how a phobia develops. Someone who had a bad experience on an airplane flight, thinks about going on another flight, and their mind pulls up the images of the past experience to help predict the risk in the current situation. The problem is, that this trait in evolutionary biology that was adaptive, in many situations is no longer useful. Factually, air travel disasters are so rare, that the likelihood of being in other, is infinitesimally small. In fact, because one survived an air disaster, they should have tremendous relief; statistically, they are not due for another one until multiple lifetimes from now meaning they can fly without impunity, they already had their unlucky experience.

As a marriage and family therapist, I see couples who have problems in their current relationship because they have mapped over the problems from their previous relationship. One couple I worked with, Bob and Bertha, always fought about money. Bertha had grown up with nothing, her family had come to America as refugees when she was very small, and she remembered growing up with almost nothing. Bob was an insurance executive, he had done very well and planned their financial future well. He bought a variety of investments, but knowing there were many years left to invest, he did put some of his resources in aggressive and even speculative investments. He felt secure knowing he had a fully funded annuity and other assets. But Bertha was determined that they would just buy houses as an investment, and believed real estate was the only sure thing since you can actually walk into it and stand on it, even if the economy goes bad. Her parents had overcome a lot, that is what they told her. They first bought a small convenience store, then an apartment for the family, and then other apartment's as investments.

Bertha was mapping her previous experiences into her current situation, and the result was a husband who felt his professional skills were not respected, a wife who was willing to have an undiversified investment portfolio, She was feeling ignored and that her experience was not being respected. As a result the fights were being escalated..

The mind only knows how to do what the mind knows how to do. We learn a lot from our family of origin. If, in your family of origin. there was physical abuse, emotional abuse, neglect, addiction, incarceration, or any number of other traumas, when you are 30 years old and no longer a kid, your mind will still instantly scan your previous experiences looking to make predictions. It will still do this when you are 50 years old, and 70 years old. This is how the mind works.

But not only does the mind scan the past to assess where we are now, it then jumps the shark and goes off into the future, predicting the future. This is the heart of many of our problems. After millions of years of human evolution, we have a subconscious mind that can, in any new situation, assess decades of previous experience and learning and then make a predictive computation of the next 5 years, and give us a behavioral or emotional action strategy in literally seconds.

It really is amazing! But unless there is a bear in the forest, or some other new threat that requires instant action, it actually is a mind trap. It is a mind trap because making financial decisions, in the case of Bob and Bertha, security requires far more than just knowing how our parents overcame adversity. What worked for her parents, in their world, with their opportunities, is probably far different from what this couple needs in this situation.

Years ago, when I was a grad student, I worked in a large car dealership where I sold Hondas. Every night, I would have to go down to the business office which had their own building to make copies. It was the second shift, and the employees were gone for the night except one clerk who answered the phone, staffed the morning shifts, and took care of notifying each department of personnel changes that would take place the next day. She was handling the second shift stuff for the service department, the new and used car departments, and the business office.

I had to walk by her desk to get to the copy machine. But she never seemed too pleased I was in her space. She was not friendly, she rarely spoke to me, and just seemed irritated that I was in the office when nobody else would come in for hours, letting her do her work without interruption. After several months of this, I finally had the courage to speak to her. I remember walking up to her desk and telling her my name, that I worked in new cars, and that after work at 10 pm, I would be eating dinner at a nearby restaurant. I asked her to dinner.

To my surprise, and without excitement, she agreed to meet me for dinner. We moved from co-workers to after work eating-buddies and eventually to a lifelong friendship. In one of those early dinners she told me about her life. I often wondered why she had such a depressing job, at the end of a long dark hallway, without any personal contact with her coworkers. As a kid her mother and father had divorced, her father was alcoholic and abusive. She told me one story about when she wanted to go to a childhood birthday party, but he was busy drinking, and so she cried. The result was she got hit. What she learned from her father was, stay quiet, stay in your room, don't talk to people and you won't get hurt. It was a strategy that saved her as a kid, but mapping it into her adult world has been less than successful even to this day.

What did you learn in your time of trauma? Did you learn relationships are not worth the risk? Did you learn problems always get worse? Did you learn to eat or drink your way to emotional numbness? When our minds scan the past and predict the future giving us a strategy to act on in that moment of decision, the action is often a result of these mind traps and the actions are not any good. The alcoholic for example, is not drinking because it makes them feel better, in fact, they know if makes them feel worse.

They are drinking for two reasons: The body's physiological craving for alcohol (put enough of a substance in your body over a long enough period of time and it will demand more of it), coupled with an obsession of the mind (to paraphrase the book Alcoholics Anonymous). It is not that alcohol makes the alcoholic feel better, it just makes them feel different. The emotional pain they are blocking out does not feel good. And neither do the consequences of their drinking, but they do it time after time, because it makes them feel different.

In the world of computer programming there is a phrase: "Garbage in, garbage out." If your brain is scanning previous traumas looking for the best action in the present, but the present is either not a trauma, a different type of difficulty, or an entirely new situation, it is going to give you garbage for a response. It is going to tell you to respond with anger, depression and anxiety. Respond with irresponsibility, respond with avoidance, and respond with self-harm.

Projecting the future

We tend to spend almost all of our mental energy either scanning the past, often with regret for the past, or predicting the future and worrying about outcomes. We regret what others have done to us, and the choices we have made along the way that ,in retrospect, did not help us. We scan the past because trauma has trained that hypothalamic-pituitary-adrenal axis to be hypervigilant and always alert.

When our minds are not scanning the past, it almost always jumps into the future and starts making predictions. A lot of us then get caught up in the fears of the future based on the activated hypothalamic-pituitary-adrenal axis. We start to dread tomorrow, or see every relationship failing, or our business collapsing, and our health failing. We guess how other people will respond to us and we try to outsmart them, both in business and our families. We try to gain control in any way we can since we can predict the future and need to mitigate disaster.

As part of my therapeutic work with couples, I do deal with financial planning. I have many couples that are so worried about the future that they are missing any joy in the moment. And I have worked with penny-pinchers who have died rich, having never enjoyed their wealth because they were so fearful of not having it.

This pattern maps over into relationships. I see people who never trust their spouse, even though there is no reason not too, and their demand for self-reliance keeps them from ever truly coupling. The result? Divorce. I see it time after time.

Researchers have determined that more than 85% of what we worry about never happens. In the 15% of occurrences when a worry did occur, almost 80% of the people reported they were able to handle it without distress. We believe what we worry about is rational and possible, and that by worrying we can create a plan that beats the crisis. But what we are really doing is missing the moment where change can take place because we are planning for a future that in all probability is not going to exist.

Anxiety and worry take not only a mental toll, but a physical toll as well. Almost every measure of health is reduced when people live in a state of anxiety.

These powerful mind traps, both dwelling and ruminating on the past, and projecting the future, are the way evolution has wired us. They say that repeat experiences code these coping strategies, both positive and negative in our minds forever. It is almost always summarized as, "What fires together, wires together." If every time you get angry you drink, every time you get angry you will drink. You can't not do it. It is how you have wired your body and your mind.

Traumas change biology, and belief. It makes these mind traps extremely difficult to overcome. We are literally, trying to rewire the brain and go against evolution. The good news though; We don't need surgery to rewire the brain, and in the next chapters I will share a proven strategy to rewire the brain and therefore change the trajectory of your life, no matter how difficult the traumas were.

CHAPTER THREE:

Freedom and Love

I live in Nevada. When recreational marijuana use became legal, and pot could be purchased as easily and openly as alcohol, a visiting friend who I grew up with said to me, "Dude, we should go buy some weed and smoke up like we were in high school!" I laughed. I understood the novelty of it, and the desire to reminisce about the past and the temptation to relive high school memories (they do call it high school for a reason).

"No," I told him, "you can try it. But I do not even drink, and I'm not interested in smoking weed – even if it's legal."

He seemed surprised. "You don't even want to try it? Why not?" he asked. "You can't get in trouble for it here now!" he exclaimed with enthusiasm.

"I don't drink, and I am not going to smoke pot for the same reason. I love life, and I don't want to miss any of it by being drunk or stoned."

For me, I did not actually quit drinking. I still drink tea. I also drink water. Once in a while I do go wild and even have a Coca-Cola. What happened when I got sober in 1988 was a transformation. I went from trying to avoid life by being drunk or stoned, to loving life. Ever since that time, I have not wanted to miss any of it by being drunk. I don't even want to miss life by being restless, irritable, or discontent. I also don't want to miss life by being depressed, anxious, or angry.

Today, despite my own adult traumas and adverse childhood experiences, I have found joy in everyday life. My hope is that by reading this book and practicing the principles contained in this book you too will find joy in everyday life. I have shared these ideas and techniques in therapy with many clients. I am confident that when you practice the ideas contained herein, you will discover this same joy.

Years ago, I was walking down Khreschatyk Street in Kiev, Ukraine. It was the last night of a ten-day trip. Khreschatyk street is where the market is, its where the subway is, and it is the area where Maiden is. It is an amazing and opulent street, with street performers on every corner, people walking, kids playing, and fountains displaying their beauty next to colorful buildings with old-world charm.

As we walked, my friend, who had never met an American before, asked me, "Are Americans like Ukrainians?" I didn't answer right away. I thought about it. I had been all over Europe, I had been to many places in Ukraine, and I speak enough Russian to get around. After another block or two of walking and pondering the question, I finally replied. "Yes, Ukrainians are just like

Americans. In fact, I have been all over the world. And people everywhere are the same. They all want two things: Love and freedom."

In the previous chapters I defined trauma, and shared how the long lasting effects of trauma can affect us for decades to come, both mentally and physically. From this point forward, I am going to be sharing how you can reverse the effect of trauma and discover both freedom and love in your life. I am going to share ideas you can activate immediately that will bring you joy and keep you from carrying the heavy burden of suffering.

Freedom

Freedom is not only a political concept, or human rights concept, but also a personal concept. We want to feel free in in almost every area of life. This is called agency. It is the ability to create and influence outcomes in our life. This would include finances, relationships, career and pursuits of happiness. Trauma impacts us by restricting our freedom. It causes self-doubt, it causes anxiety, it leads us to believe that we have limitations, and that others control our outcomes.

Freedom and agency go hand in hand. When we have self-efficacy, the ability to do things on our own or from within, we have both agency and freedom. It gives us an ability to act with intentionality, to pursue our quests in our own way.

Freedom decreases stress. People who have financial freedom do not worry about day to day bills. People who have freedom in their relationships do not worry a love will be lost. People who have freedom in their career do not feel like they are "working for the man." People who have freedom feel unrestricted in their pursuits and the outcome of this freedom is an ability to be self-directed.

I have worked with clients with catastrophic health conditions. These have ranged from HIV, to cancer, and kidney failure. I have a good friend who spent years on dialysis before his transplant. He felt his daily dialysis sessions took away his freedom. Not only his freedom to travel or be away form home, but his freedom to live without worry. I worked with HIV positive individuals in the early days of the AIDS epidemic. They feet trapped by the diagnosis, and that their freedom had been taken. (Fortunately, modern HIV treatments have resulted in restoring a sense of freedom in many patients.)

How have your traumas restricted your sense of freedom and agency? As a kid who endured emotional abuse, do you now question your every move? Did the abusive relationship between your parents, restrict your ability to be normal in your relationships? Trauma steals freedom.

How do you create personal freedom after trauma? You can begin today with these three ideas:

1. **Act without permission.** Trauma survivors often ask for permission to take action. They do it both verbally and non-verbally. In a marriage, they might ask their spouse, "Can I do this, or can I do that?" As if they are still seeking parental approval. Of course,

spouses should communicate, especially on big mutual decisions, but in many cases individuals give up their identity by seeking permission for mundane, or daily activities. Even on the bigger issues, retain your autonomy, you are an equal participant in the direction of your family.

Non-verbally we ask for permission by second guessing our actions. We ask for permission by failing to take action without the recognition of others. I am an active member in several writers clubs. I meet people who fall into one of two types; one - they write a book because they want to get it done and publish it, then they start selling books, become excited by success and write some more; two - there is the person who for years has been "working" on something and they pass around excerpts asking for feedback, and writing and revising a hundred times before publishing, waiting for validation before publishing, but even then, most of these people never publish. What the later lacks is not ideas or skills. In fact, those who are publishing are often less skilled and inferior writers. What they have, is the ability to act without permission.

2. **Put your own oxygen mask on first, before helping others**. It has been my observation that people with a history of trauma are often the first to help others. Perhaps this comes from a desire to spare others pain they have experienced, or perhaps it comes from the desire to be needed, or to meet some other

psychological need. You have taken a great step towards putting your own oxygen mask on first by reading this book.

The reason we must put on our own oxygen mask first, before we help our spouse, our children or anyone else traveling in this journey of life with us is so that we are strong enough to begin what we have started, and have the ability to guide others through experience. Freedom comes by taking care of our own essential needs. If we do not do this first, what happens is we set up a trap for failure and more self-punishment. When you first practice this, you may feel you are not giving enough, or that you are being selfish, but soon, as you "oxygenate" your own life first, you will discover you have real freedom, and an ability to help others from a position of wellness.

3. **Seek and value long-term rewards.** Ultimately, it may feel free to do what you want to, anything from drugs, to quitting a job on the spur of the moment, or doing anything that involves short-term rewards, but in the long-term this has consequences. Shopping on a credit card, exacting revenge with a quick word, or skipping a needed car repair because it means taking time out of a busy day, are all things that may seem to decrease stress or bring freedom in the moment, but clearly, there are long term consequences for any of these things.

People with a history of trauma often seek out the immediate reward. In the science of trauma, it provides a blast of powerful brain chemicals that feel good in the moment, but real freedom comes from shifting thinking to long-term rewards. Getting drunk out of anger might seem like it feels good tonight but waking up in jail with huge fines for public intoxication, might end your job, crush your finances and cause family problems. Ask yourself, "Is the reward for this decision short-term or long-term?" If there is no long term-reward and there are real risks, decide to put off the action until later.

Note, I did not say, don't do it. Give yourself freedom by simply delaying any action. You still retain the agency to act in anyway you want to, but now you are practicing making better choices. Of course, some actions can take away our freedom. Start paying attention to this. Credit cards crush finances, rage complicates parenting, drug abuse can have legal or work-related consequences.

It is hard to shift choices if lifetime patterns are being changed. This is the time to increase your freedom by asking others for support, or reaching out to a professional therapist to help create new patterns.

Love

How do we amplify love and both love ourselves and others following trauma? To this point, love may seem elusive. In replicating past traumas, there may be a string of broken relationships, some through our own doing and some from putting ourselves in situations where we were hurt time after time.

I think learning to love ourselves is the first step. It requires being gentle to ourselves. Gentleness means we stop being self-critical and start noticing our strengths. Almost all of us know exactly what is wrong with us. We know our character defects, we know our weaknesses. Often though, we have neglected to define ourselves by our strengths. This is the first step in loving ourselves. Ask yourself, "What is right with me?" You can acknowledge, "Hey, I have a lot of problems." But take a moment right now and ask yourself these things:

- What am I good at?
- What are my resources?
- What are the personality characteristics I have that will help me?
- What do I do right?

Stop and pause right now, and really answer these four questions. There are answers to them. It may have been so long since you looked at what is right with you that its hard to answer these four simple questions, but when you take the time do so, you will have taken the first step towards being gentle on yourself and paying attention to why you are worthy of love.

The answers yield justifications for loving yourself and justifications for others to love you. Practice accepting love. Is it a pattern for you to discount or reject compliments of others? Start accepting them with a simple, "Thank-you."

For some readers, the following advise will seem trite,

or too simplistic. I want you to try it anyway. When was the last time you were hugged in a meaningful way? The science behind hugging is proven. Hugs can reduce pain, both physical and psychological. Hugs cause us to release oxytocin, which can impact our stress level and reduce blood pressure.

Wrapping your arms around your midsection, as if you were hugging yourself can have the same impact. Hug yourself now. Wrap your arms around your midsection. It might feel silly. It might even feel uncomfortable. Perhaps it will feel wonderful. But do it now. Hold yourself for ten seconds.

Bring yourself to an empowered place with your own hug. Now, do this with intention 12 times a day. Every hour on the hour. Do it for ten seconds. It is the physical connection to yourself that you need to truly start loving yourself. (Note: The sillier you think this is, or the more uncomfortable and difficult it is to do this, the greater the likelihood is that you need to do this.)

Loving others

It may be hard to love others. You may have been wronged by so many people in so many traumatic situations, that you have become an island. A rock. Simon and Garfunkel wrote a song that rose to the top of the charts called, *I am a Rock*. A song becomes number one because people identify with it. It was a number one song.

The lyrics were, "I am a rock. I am an island, and a

rock feels no pain, and an island never cries." I understand loving other people might not be a point you are at right now, but included in my website at www.TurnAroundTrauma.com is a great loving-kindness meditation and when you download it and practice it you are going to discover, it is possible to begin loving others again. Go ahead, download it from my website now. It is free to access.

As mentioned, throughout this book I am going to share short ideas like these that an be helpful to you. Not all of these ideas will resonate with you. Not all of these ideas will apply to you, or be possible. But there are many ideas in this book and they will become progressively more actionable. By picking out some of them and taking action on them, you will begin to discover a new manor of living. It will be powerful.

CHAPTER FOUR:

Acceptance, Distancing, Defusion, Resilience

This chapter is going to teach you a three-step process for moving from trauma and adverse experience to joy. The following chapters are going to give you specific tools for doing this. Did you notice I have not used any of these common phrases?

- Take control of trauma or adverse experiences
- Resolve trauma or adverse experiences
- End trauma or adverse experiences
- Beat trauma or adverse experiences

Acceptance

The reason is simple. We cannot do anything about the past. It cannot be changed, it cannot be beat, it cannot be resolved, and it is already over. The only moment we have is right now. Too often in the world of psychology there is a desire to revisit trauma, re-experience trauma, or oven "take control of trauma." The only thing we can actually do about previous trauma is accept it. When I tell clients we are going to accept our traumas and adverse childhood experiences, they often revolt. "How can I accept childhood sexual abuse?" they earnestly ask, "Are you telling me I need to feel like I wanted it?"

Other clients say, "Accept my mother's actions? She rejected her own child! She failed to protect me. She even hurt me! I will never accept her." I understand that the word acceptance can conjure up the idea of liking something or it can seem I am asking a person to open communication with someone who is not safe to invite back into their life. But this is not what acceptance is about.

Acceptance is about putting space between our current experience and the past. It is about saying, "That was then, this is now." The big book of alcoholics puts it quite eloquently when it says:

"And acceptance is the answer to all my problems today. When I am disturbed, it is because I find some person, place, thing, or situation as being, unacceptable to me, and I can find no serenity until I accept that person, place, thing, or situation as being exactly as it is in this moment."

The book continues: "Until I could accept my alcoholism, I could not stay sober; unless I accept life completely on life's terms I cannot be happy. I need to concentrate not so much on what needs to be changed in the world as on what needs to be changed in me and my attitudes." *[I have taken a literary liberty and paraphrased the quote, eliminating a religious message in the original quote that others my find helpful, but that I have not found to be a requirement for acceptance.]*

There is a lot to unpack in this passage, but it is the best understanding of acceptance I have ever seen. I love how the first line stays focused on problems of today. In the past we all had many problems, but the only problems we need to handle are todays. There is a saying, "How do you eat an elephant? One bit at a time." In dealing with the many adverse experiences we have had, the only bite we need to take is todays. There is no need to go backwards to rehash old wounds, or even to solve problems of the future that have not yet arrived. By staying in today, you actually not only increase acceptance, but freedom as well.

"Is" is a word with only two letters. But it is one of the most powerful words in our language. It is small but mighty. Say these phrases out loud:

It is.

It just is.

It is finished.

Each of these simple sentences convey the idea of acceptance, and when we can see our previous traumas as they are, then they become something that is. That means they are something we can just see. Something we can just feel. Something we can just acknowledge. No longer do we need to control these things, or even attach meaning to them. We can just let them be what they "is."

When I was young my mother always explained bad things with a trite phrase, "Everything happens according to God's plan." This is actually a common way of trying to accept things. Another common way we are told to accept is to understand, "God's got a purpose." These ideas didn't help me accept, they just made me angry – and angry at a god who would take away a kid's father. These were some of my thoughts, did you ever have similar thoughts?

"My dad left us? That was God's plan?"

"My dad just died from his addiction, and god planned it?"

I think my religious upbringing actually kept me from understanding what real acceptance was. And acceptance just is. It is nothing more, it is nothing less. Sometimes it feels better, sometimes it doesn't. And that is ok. Sometimes I understand, and sometimes I remain confused. But at least I accept.

I have shared this exercise with many clients over the years in my therapy office. They find it helps them to accept. To see, "that person, place, thing, or situation as being exactly as it is in this moment", requires seeing things from the past in the present moment and moving to a point where it just "is." No explanation required.

I have my clients close their eyes. I tell them that they can take as long as they want to go through this process. I tell them they do not have to like or dislike it. They do not have to have any particular emotions about this, and that they can even feel indifferent or detached. I tell them this exercise will not change the past, nor cause them to wish it on others. Merely, it will help them accept. You can follow the same process in your mind as you read along:

> Imagine you are in a large conference room with chairs surrounding a large table. You are sitting in the executive chair at the end and all of the other chairs remain unoccupied. Alone in the room, you notice a large box that sits in the middle of the table. Acceptance does not mean you like something. Nor does it mean you wish it would happen again or happen to others. Acceptance simply means a willingness to see that which has occupied your thoughts, feelings, or concerns, and to acknowledge the role these things have played in your life.
>
> The box on the table holds all of those things that you have not wanted to look at. Perhaps you have not wanted to see these things because of pain, fear, or for some other reason. However, in this office you are safe and you have come here to move forward. In the safety of this office is your opportunity to begin unpacking these things and placing them on the table. One by one, unpack those items from the box, looking at them.
>
> Without judgment or attachment, place them on the table. See yourself taking each item out and simply placing them on the table. When the box is unpacked, look at all of those items. Rather than sitting again, simply stand at the end of the table.

Take as much time as needed to simply see them out on the table. You are safe and you are the only person in the room observing the table. When you have looked long enough at all of the items on the table, imagine that you approach the doorway, leaving those items exposed. Turn out the light. Walk through the door, closing it behind you.

Those things, feelings, and experiences are neither hidden nor neglected. As you walk out the door and into the light of this new chapter of life, recognize they were there. By living fully in the present, you have developed a sense of acceptance, simply seeing life as it is and practicing the new art of living in the moment.

Distancing

Distancing is the art of putting space between us and our emotions. We can also put space between us and our experiences, our thoughts, and our sensations. The problem most of us have is that we become our emotions. There is no "space" between us and our emotions. Have you said to yourself? "I am sad!" or "I am hurt?" or "I am angry?" Of course you have. But the problem here is that when you say to yourself that you are angry, you become anger. It joins with you and literally becomes you. You have certainly heard someone say, "They are just an angry person." The person who is being referred to has the identity of anger, their personhood and their anger are one and the same.

A hallmark of emotionally intelligent people is the

ability to put space between themselves and their emotions. They are a person who is angry, not an angry person. A person who is angry is angry for a measure of time or in a specific situation, but the person who is an angry person is that all of the time. It's a subtle language distance, but you can see the difference don't you?

They say time heals all wounds. Actually, it doesn't. Like, "all things work to good for the glory of God" the phrase "time heals all wounds" is actually untrue also. But what time can do is put space between you and your traumas. Time is another way of distancing. All to often though, time has passed since the adverse experience but the emotions are still raw, still present and can emerge with as much force as if the experience happened yesterday. What this tells us is that while time can be our friend, other methods of distancing need to be employed.

Research shows that one of the most powerful ways to put some space between you and your emotions, you and your thoughts, and you and your sensations is with the practice of mindfulness. The next chapter is devoted specifically to what I think, and the research supports, is one of the most effective skills you can learn to move from trauma to acceptance, and eventually into resilience.

The research shows that parents who practice mindfulness, raise happier kids, have better marriages, and find greater satisfaction in life. Their kids grow up better able to handle difficult situations and if you are a parent who learns mindfulness you can break the cycle of adverse childhood experiences by mastering this single technique.

There are many ways to distance. Some people have chosen to leave a toxic family behind and move across the country, or even the globe. The problem with this strategy, is that no matter where you go you have to take yourself with you, and no matter how far you move physically, until you can put some distance between you and your thoughts, you and the pain of those relationships, even 7000 miles away, it is still with us.

The US military understands the value of mindfulness. Programs have been developed to help soldiers overcome PTSD by practicing being fully in the present and putting space between them and their traumas. The US military has also found that by proactively training soldiers in mindfulness, they decrease adverse response to stressful situations that soldiers often face, especially during times of war or other military conflict.

Right now you can begin putting space between your traumas and you as a person by taking a breath, paying attention to that breath, and feeling this book between your fingers. Practice paying attention deliberately to only this moment. The air in the room around you, the place where you sit. Set aside yesterday, you do not have to regret yesterday or even shut the door on it, just acknowledge it is there and use your awareness of the past as a cue to bring your attention to the present moment. Suspend following your thoughts into the future, and questioning if an activity like this will actually be helpful. Just breath. Pay attention to this moment and your awareness of all that this moment contains. Focus on this for the next 60 seconds, not following your emotions, thoughts or sensations , just letting them be whatever they are and bringing your attention to the present moment.

Now that 60 seconds is up, do you notice anything different? It is probly not an earth-shattering awareness of wild abundance. That would be a pretty dramatic response. But do you notice by practicing the skill of being in this moment, you put some space between you and the traumas of the past. Do you feel the distance? Mindfulness is an effective strategy for distancing.

Cognitive defusion

George Bernard Shaw said, "People become attached to their burdens sometimes more than the burdens are attached to them." Cognitive defusion is the practice of looking at our thoughts as an observer of them, rather than from our thoughts. The problem with people is that we think too much. Even when we sleep we think. Like a fish swims in water, people literally swim in thoughts. What the Shaw quote suggests is that we become our thoughts, rather than just a swimmer in them. They become something we are fused to. We have repetitive thoughts, we ruminate on our thoughts, and we "are what we think." Trauma is something you commonly rethink. The thoughts you have associated with those experiences, you may have become fused to.

Thoughts can create behavior, but they do not dictate

behavior. You can put some space between you and your thoughts by practicing the outside observer role. The steps to breaking this fusion are as follows:

1. Identify the thought you are following or cannot let go of.

2. Decide whether it is a memory, a prediction about the future, or if have you created a meaning that you have attached to the thought?

3. Practice in your own mind saying the thought out loud.

4. Practice visualizing the situation where you have this thought.

5. Create a break in your thoughts. Think about anything else. I call this a "mental saltine." Clap your hands, take in a breath to break the state or the thought associated with this visualization or the words you have spoken.

6. Now, revisit the idea again, but as an observer. Attach no meaning to what you think, see, or feel. Just observe it. Visualize yourself from a distance in this situation, hear yourself as if it is another you speaking the words, or even someone else who has said them.

7. Stay in the present, seeing this as an exercise, not going back to the actual event.

8. Practice observing, from the safety of distance.

9. You have now put some space between you and your thoughts.

10. Take a moment to see yourself as the new you, right here, with some space between you and your thoughts. Pay attention to your breath, to this moment. Do you notice at one level, big or small, more room between you and your thoughts?

Resilience

Resilience is the art of becoming strong enough both emotionally and physically to handle both psychological and physical stress with increased strength. No weightlifter can lift 10,000 pounds by him or herself. There is a breaking point, even for Olympic weightlifting champions. In the arena of adverse experiences, there are some that can break us. The good news is, that a team of weightlifters can lift 10,000 pounds, and with support you can lift any difficulty you face in the future. This is why part of your strategy needs to be becoming involved in a supportive community of likeminded people. I am a fan of support groups like Alcoholics Anonymous, non-shaming, non-judgmental religious communities, professional supports, and community involvement to help you take the resilience you create to an Olympic level.

But right now, lets start at a basic level. You will be adding mindfulness as a core strategy to putting space between you and your thoughts, feelings, and emotions. You will also use mindfulness to create resilience. By practicing mindfulness, you will be prepared for the next tough time, the next adverse experience, the next trauma to come your way. Again, I will expand on this in the next chapter.

Right now, begin cultivating resilience while you read the pages of this book by accepting these three ideas:

1. Change is the normal experience of life. Previous adverse experiences cause us to seek stability. One of our greatest needs is security. Change can be seen as a threat to security, but this causes us problems since change is the normal state of life. Open yourself to change by reassuring yourself, change is normal.

   During the last big financial crisis, a decade ago, people lost jobs. For many, this was traumatic. After securing new jobs it might have been normal for someone to say, "I am never leaving this job" because it feels secure. But the normal state is change. New opportunities arise, new economic conditions develop, and being open to riding the waves of change is a good thing. It fosters resilience.

2. Take care of your health. We are only emotionally as well as we are physically. To be resilient requires both mental strength and physical strength. Are you walking each day? Are you feeding your body nourishing food? Are you sleeping well? Resilience is fostered by basic self-care. It is a simple place to start. In fact, you can do it now. Download a pedometer app on your phone and set a daily goal. Decide to add a nutrient dense salad to every meal. This is not dieting, you are not cutting anything out, you are just adding the nutrition first. Sleep hygiene is essential. It is when both our bodies and our

minds heal, but it is also how we cultivate resilience.

3. Scale stress into perspective. When new stressors, anything ranging from a fender bender to an unexpected change, come our way, our previous experiences tell us they are going to be big deals! But this is a mind trap. Each spin on a slot machine is independent of every other spin. In other words, you have the exact same odds of winning or loosing on any spin, regardless of whether the machine is "hot" or is "due for a win."

Stressful events are like the slot machine. They are independent of our other stressors. You are anticipating big stress levels since that has been your previous experience. You can stop this by scaling your current experience into perspective. Ask yourself, "On a scale of 1-10 (with ten being the most stressful), how stressful is this current experience." The result will be an instant ability to put it into perspective, which will yield an increase in your resilience levels.

The three stages of moving out of a trauma-based experience to a foundation of freedom and love, is to first accept, then put some space between you and the past, and then develop resilience. By following this pathway, you will be far more likely to master the techniques and derive the benefit research shows has helped so many other people.

CHAPTER FIVE:

What it was like, what happened and what it's like now

What it was like

When I was growing, up my father was an unfunctional alcoholic. As a small child I thought it was great, he didn't work so he took me fishing, took me to the store to buy beer, and took me to the firehouse to hang out with the other volunteer firemen. I'm not actually sure he was sober enough to actually volunteer, but his friends were there. I was six when my parents divorced. We lived north of Chicago and my mother kept the house. My father drove away to South Texas in a U-Haul. I only saw him twice after that, once when I went to visit for a week when I was age ten, and once when his father died when I was 15. A year later he was dead, a result of his addiction. We will never really know if it was his health, suicide, or what the actual cause of death was, but he was 42 at the time and left a long list of broken promises behind.

I idolized my father. It was easy to do as a child, but

my playmate had been banished by my mother. I was angry with her for divorcing him, and she then did the best that she could to make it right by marrying the complete opposite husband.

At age ten, my two sisters and I moved into my step-fathers house with his four children. I was number 5 out of seven. It was supposed to be like the Brady Bunch, but it was more like the Twilight zone. There was raging and yelling in the house. One of my first memories of our now blended family was a family bonding trip where all nine of us piled in the 1973 Oldsmobile station wagon. It has a fold up seat in the trunk that faced the wrong direction, I was one of the three youngest, so I sat facing the wrong way. We were on a journey from Chicago to Denver, 15 hours of driving. At some point on the journey my new step-father pulled over to physically discipline his teenage son with punches not spanks.

My mother compensated for all of this by joining a fundamentalist church, and when my step-father was not busy raging, she was busy "Keeping the marriage together because Jesus wanted it that way." There were good things that happened. In many ways I was lucky, the experience of others was far more traumatic. My step-father really was the guy who walked nine miles to school in the snow, uphill, and he did teach me the value of hard work and he did support my hobby of earning money doing magic at children's birthday parties by driving me to my gigs in the same station wagon.

But the chaos in our home created uncertainty, a lack

Turn Around Trauma

of security and fear. I spent a lot of time in my room. I read a lot of books. I learned to lay low and stay out of drama. All of these were healthy coping strategies. But by the time I was 16, I was praising Jesus in the church youth group and stealing gin from their liquor cabinet. When my father died, I felt lost. The youth pastor assured me he was in hell since my father had expressed specifically to me that he was not a Christian, but assured me that when I got to heaven it would be like a baseball game. My father wouldn't be there. But I would still be happy. He said this, "It's like winning a baseball game but missing the ball in one inning. You're disappointed you didn't make the play, but you're still happy you won the game." To this day, I still think it was one of the cruelest things to say to a child, and I also now recognize it as bad theology.

I continued to drink through adolescence and into early adulthood. I was drinking until late at night, and I was drinking alone. I drank in the morning to steady my shakes, and pretty clearly, I was on the same path as my father. I got sober through Alcoholics Anonymous when I was 21. Like many counselors, I went into graduate school looking for answers to my own problems rather than to help others. I graduated, and got a job working in addiction treatment as a counselor. I always had impostor syndrome. I knew that even though I was sober (frankly, I was scared to drink, I knew I would end up in prison for drunk driving or worse, killing someone behind the wheel, or dead from suicide if I kept drinking. There were many scary nights that preceded the night I had my last drink.) I was just as messed up as all of the patients. I was lonely, I was angry, I was faking it till I could make it. I became an earnest student of self-improvement, meditation, the 12-step programs, and hypnosis and NLP. By age 30, I was now a twice married parent of unplanned children, who had largely channeled my confusion into trying to help others grasp what I seemed myself to be unable to get. People looking in at me thought I had it together, I had become an expert at hiding things, but anyone who really knew me knew me as impulsive, undisciplined, and quick to quit and move on to a new place before the gig was up.

I am obviously leaving out a lot of details, but like you, and like my clients, I had my share of adverse childhood experiences. These impacted me in my behaviors, in my ability to express emotions and clearly some of this instability I now see has impacted my relationship, trust, and sense of security for more than 50 years. My general coping strategy is to not rock the boat, to make sure others are happy first, and simply hide my real self in both professional and personal relationships.

What Happened

By my mid 30's I had parlayed my counseling experience and ability to tell stories into a successful continuing education company training other mental health professionals on issues related to addiction, family violence, and creating calm in crisis. Other therapists loved my courses, and the clients I worked with loved how genuine my teachings were. By this time in my career, since I was an avid reader, I discovered the power of mindfulness. When I taught this to my patient groups they made real changes. I wanted what they had.

My internal struggle was based on those adverse childhood experiences. I was trapped. No matter how much I learned and how much others benefitted from what I taught, I still felt insecure. I still felt ashamed to reveal the real me (even now it is difficult to share my personal story). By my late 30's, I was divorced again. Remember earlier when I talked about the importance of love? I wanted real love. I wanted to love others and accept love in return. So, I did the most logical thing I could think of, I started dating someone 7000 miles away. That would be safe!

Every day we wrote emails and exchanged snail-mail. It was a perfect relationship for me. I could show up every three months for a week and spend the rest of my time hiding behind the newly invented internet. Of course, I picked someone who was looking for an overseas relationship for probaly the same reasons I was.

Soon, I found myself on a charter boat ride in the South China Sea, which was a perk for staying as a guest at a resort hotel with my date. The vessel was a tiny sailboat. It was operated by a life-long fisherman who earned extra money giving rides to hotel guests. Before we got on this boat, I thought to myself, "Hey those clouds don't look so great."

Having lived in tornado country all my life, I

understand what dangerous clouds look like, but he assured me everything was fine. Trusting that he was a professional and an expert in local weather, I got in the boat against my better judgment. Before long, the sky grew darker, and the seas got rougher. It soon became clear that he had lost control of the boat, and we were in danger. As each wave doused us with powerful blasts of water and the rain began to hit my face, I started to panic.

I knew I was way too far out to swim back to land, and the seas were so rough, I surely would have been swallowed up anyway if I jumped overboard. When I looked at the boat captain, this man of the sea, and I saw fear in his eyes, I knew death was soon to arrive. We drifted further and further from land and as control over the boat became nearly impossible, I could feel my body shaking in panic.

In my own mind, I saw anguished images of my children, mourning my death and asking why I was on the darn boat ride in the first place. I felt sad. I was fearful. I looked backwards and forwards wondering if I should jump.

I looked to the sky, and suddenly I got pelted by this huge raindrop. It was a giant, and it was hot. It was a big, hot raindrop. It was tropical rain, so it was salty and hot. With the boat moving, each raindrop splashed with a full force, the heat stinging my face. And it was in that moment that I really felt the drops, the salt, the heat, and the force of the rain, and it truly hurt. The sea was white below my seat. It was a mesh seat, and the water was splashing underneath me as the wind blew ferociously. As I felt those things, I realized in my thoughts that I'm going to die. And I thought, "I don't want to die on this boat. I'm not ready to die today!"

The thought of my kids continued to pass through my mind. I could even see them standing with frowns and tears in my memorial service, just like I did at my fathers, and I was really suffering anguish on this boat with death probably just a few minutes away - and then I got hit by another raindrop, hot and salty.

And again, I noticed it and I said, "That was hot." In noticing that, I recognized at that moment that what I had always told my clients was true. No matter what else is going on if you're breathing, this moment is okay. So, I breathed, and unintentionally I did what I have asked my clients to do in difficult situations: I took another breath.

I didn't try to speed up or slow down the breath. I just breathed. And again, I breathed, paying attention to the wet, salty breath. I noticed my fear, as well as my powerlessness over my fear, and I learned what acceptance was, simply accepting my fear as fear. I took another breath, breathing in, breathing out, fearful but breathing, breathing each breath into each moment that was left. Soon I noticed the feeling of the waves below my seat, the feeling of the wind on my face, and in that moment, I was amazed by the beauty of the rough churning seas despite the impending doom that they would bring. I breathed again, and I felt the hot rain. I hardly noticed when I stopped following my thoughts of panic, and I just experienced each moment not knowing which one would be the last. Then I noticed that my heart rate had slowed. Although my panic was there it became unimportant because I paid no attention to it. I accepted death, simply noting my awareness of mortality, and in that moment, I felt human. I felt a part of the sea.

And I just breathed again, and I understood Mindfulness experientially, connecting each moment in just being okay.

I still have no idea how the boat captain got the boat under control but, somehow, we made it to a small little island, and we were safe. We stayed there for a long period of time on the shore. We just sat in the rain. I breathed again, paying attention to the breath that one single moment - and I smiled.

And this is what will happen to you when you learn to experience the moment and let go of the past and stop analyzing the future. There will come a point where what you have been practicing becomes something you own. Every time I teach Mindfulness to clients, none of them say, "Wow, that was earth shattering and dramatic: that was just crazily life-changing." They almost all say, "That was okay. I can see how that can be helpful." Or they might say, "Yeah, I found that relaxing." But after practicing Mindfulness every day, there will come a time where they'll recognize and realize that they have been intuitively mindful. It's at that moment that you will own Mindfulness - and you will own Mindfulness from that point forward as well.

What it's like now

My ability to be mindful, rather than just teach mindfulness has improved every day since that day on the boat in the South China sea. Since that time, I have tested the ability of mindfulness to steady my course, and to provide enough space between me and my thoughts, my feelings and my pain. A few years ago, I went through a serious health scare. But by that point mindfulness had become a way of life for me. I had finally got what my clients in therapy got. My teaching is not only smart and filled with ideas people love, but its genuine. I feel like I can finally share, not just what the textbooks say, and not just what I have seen in my client's lives, but from real changes in me that have transformed my adverse childhood experiences into something I can now accept.

Today, my finances are in order, my relationships are good, and my stress induced health problems are long gone. I can see how my experiences can benefit others.

I hesitated to write this chapter, to put my story which I have carefully guarded out in the public. The reason I am sharing it is that I want you to know that it is never too late to transform trauma into joy, and to create security and significance. I no longer have impostor syndrome. I no longer regret the past, nor wish to shut the door on it.

The book *Alcoholics Anonymous* has a section referred to as the promises. When you really understand the concepts in the next chapter, and practice them until they are real, I am quite certain that you will experience them too. The 12-steps really do embody the idea of Mindfulness quite well. Here they are:

"If we are painstaking about this phase of our development, we will be amazed before we are halfway through. We are going to know a new freedom and a new happiness. We will not regret the past nor wish to shut the door on it. We will comprehend the word serenity and we will know peace. No matter how far down the scale we have gone, we will see how our experience can benefit others. That feeling of uselessness and self-pity will disappear. We will lose interest in selfish things and gain interest in our fellows. Self-seeking will slip away. Our whole attitude and outlook upon life will change. Fear of people and of economic insecurity will leave us. We will intuitively know how to handle situations which used to baffle us. We will suddenly realize that God is doing for us what we could not do for ourselves.

Are these extravagant promises? We think not. They are being fulfilled among us—sometimes quickly, sometimes slowly. They will always materialize if we work for them."

CHAPTER SIX:

Making Mindfulness Real

The Great Master Oogway gave us these powerful words: "Yesterday is history, tomorrow is a mystery, all we have is the present, that is why it is a gift." You may recognize Master Oogway as the turtle from the Kung Fu Panda movies. How can a cartoon turtle possibly have the answer to how to change everything? Because he taught mindfulness. Mindfulness is the strategy and practice of training our minds to stop scanning the past and projecting into the future. It is a simple method of being fully in the present. For those who have been tormented by the traumas of the past, this simple action become a gift. A lifechanging gift.

Mindfulness is a well-researched approach to putting some space between you and your thoughts, feelings, and sensations. It has been found to reduce stress, control pain (both physical and emotional) and help us break the mind traps of dwelling on the past or worrying about the future.

A simple and profound truth is that no matter what

we are experiencing, no matter what the problem, no matter how difficult things are, as long as we are breathing we are actually okay. The simple logic we can extend from this is that each breath defines each moment and in each moment we are actually okay.

I have discussed mindfulness throughout this book, shared some examples and in the previous chapter I shared my own story. I am devoting this chapter to the process of making mindfulness real. In other words, how you can derive all of the proven benefits of mindfulness. Trauma changes our brains. It wires together events that have fired together. In other words, you brain has been trained by adverse life experiences to respond in certain ways. It is beyond the scope and purpose of this book to discuss the science of it, but on my website at www.TurnAroundTrauma.com I have some additional resources that will help you understand how trauma affects us not only emotionally, but how it physically codes responses into our brains.

In my TEDx talk, I called this the shark in the water. The shark in the water is the idea that no matter how we want to change automatic responses and behavioral patterns we keep repeating them because it literally is what our brain chemistry is commanding us to do.

It is true that alcoholism is a physical condition. Our bodies literally crave that which is killing us. The alcoholic body processes alcohol different than the non-alcoholic, and both the presence of adverse childhood experiences and genetics play a role in why some people are alcoholics and others are not. This is probably true for people who rage, people who are depressed and people who have any other host of problems they need to overcome. Obesity is driven by both psychological and physiological factors. Loneliness is hardwired, as is anxiety. We can in fact, at least partly, blame biology.

But the good news is that changing the brain does not require brain surgery. Study after study shows that by practicing Mindfulness we create new associations in the brain, and we literally change brain structure. We move from evolutionary responses to intentional responses. We can change the brain. We can rewire associations and responses. We can establish a new course no matter where we come from.

What it requires is practice. The daily practice of mindfulness. Just like an athlete must practice for the game so that when under pressure during the big race they can perform at their best, we must practice mindfulness so that we can perform in a way that is best. By practicing, we are changing our brains, putting space between us and our thoughts, and preparing to step into a new chapter of life where we respond to everything differently.

To make mindfulness real you must want to change. By reading this book to this point you have clearly made that decision. Now commit to practicing mindfulness each and every day. The good news here is that unlike the gym, mindfulness does not take hours of practice each day. And unlike the gym that requires we get in our car and drive to a special place with weights, aerobic machines, and Zumba classes, we can actually practice

Mindfulness anywhere and at any time.

I am going to share a couple of ways to do this. These should be your starting points. On my website at nongard.com/aces I have additional resources you can access for free that will help you in your daily practice.

I have never had a client yet who thought these beginning strategies were life changing or profound when they first began. But the clients who did trust the process and follow my instructions for 21 days, almost always at some point came back with a huge smile, recognizing in retrospect the value of the practice.

They say that sharpening an axe does not fell a tree. But by sharpening the axe, it is far easier to fell the tree when you get to the forest.

The idea of Mindfulness and staying in the moment might sound simple, but these are skills that need to be taught to a client. It is not something that happens organically just because they come to therapy each week. A big part of the homework that I assign to my clients is to practice two minutes of Mindfulness, with intention, every day between now and their next session. By the way, that's the great thing about Mindfulness. It's not about meditating for thirty minutes while assuming special postures or wearing unique clothes. In fact, a person doesn't even need to be still to practice Mindfulness. You can mindfully shop at the grocery store. You can mindfully walk. You can mindfully be still in a chair for some time, and you can mindfully eat raisins. Mindfulness is not about a specific style or vantage point of meditation, and it certainly is not about clearing one's mind. The goal in Mindfulness is not to empty one's mind or to stop thinking. On the contrary, it is to simply to give us time to allow ourselves to observe ourselves swimming in our thoughts, in the moment.

A Basic Mindfulness Meditation

While you could read volumes about Mindfulness, the best way to learn about it is to experience it. I will provide a script like the process I use with my clients; to truly learn about Mindfulness, you should, with intention, practice Mindfulness every day, twice a day for the next seven days. That's the same assignment that I give my clients, and I guarantee that if you do the assignment then you will find what my clients find: when they cultivate Mindfulness, the value of it is incredible.

Like an athlete or musician, practice is for a performance. Mindfulness meditation is our daily practice for living life to its greatest potential.

There are three components to the practice:

- First, the practice of directing your attention to your breath.

- Second, practicing how to return your attention to your breath anytime you notice feelings, thoughts or sensations. The goal is not to stop thinking, stop feeling or to stop having sensations. The purpose is to simply note when you do this and to practice bringing your attention back to a focal point, in this case the breath.

- The third part of this practice is to begin to notice how easy and natural it is to stay in the present when we notice our attention drifting into either the past or the future. Notice, during this week, times when you mindfully and intuitively return from distressing thoughts, feelings, or sensations back to your breath into the present.

As you sit in your chair with your body relaxed and your posture in alignment, close your eyes and breath in noticing what it feels like to breathe in.

Scan your body and loosen any muscles that are holding tension. Relax the jaw and let the shoulders drop and you can let your eyelids and hands feel heavy with relaxation as you just breathe. You don't have to try to speed up or slow down the breath during this exercise. All you need to do is breath and pay attention to your breath. There's not really a right way or a wrong way to do this practice. It is simply the practice of bringing your attention to your breath when you notice it wandering off.

Observe the breath, noticing the tempo of your breath, the temperature of the air, and the way you breathe. Observe how the air flows in, and what it feels like to flow out. We breathe every moment of the day, most of the time without noticing it, and by practicing paying attention to it, we are really practicing attention to this moment. Each breath marks each moment, and the only moment we actually have is this movement. No matter what stress we have endured, or are now enduring, at a basic level as long as we're breathing in this moment, we're okay.

As you breathe in and out, label the breath. Call it by its name. Label the in - breath "in" and call the out-breath "out.". Say to yourself, "in" and "out". Notice the air as you breathe in and the point where the air in your lungs turns around and becomes an exhale. As you pay attention to the breath, you'll also notice you are aware of sounds, sensations, and experiences apart from your breath

The practice is not to stop noticing those things, but rather when you notice thoughts and awareness's outside of the task of paying attention to the breath, simply note that you are doing that and return your attention to the breath.

If you notice yourself thinking about anything at all, you don't have to try to stop thinking; rather just note the thought instead of following it. Simply say to yourself that "this is a thought." Bring your attention back to the breath. If you become aware of an emotion or a feeling during this time, it's okay to have them. The practice here is not to suppress them, but not to follow them, to simply note them and say "that is a feeling" and return your attention to the breath.

Likewise, if you have any sensations, if your body feels something, you can simply note, "that is what my body feels, that is a sensation or experience", and without becoming engaged in it or following it just use it as a cue to return your attention to the breath noticing what it feels like to breathe in and out . Over the next two minutes, continue to breathe in and out paying attention to your breath. By practicing being an observer of the breath, you can apply this skill of observation to your traumas, to your adverse life experiences, and see them from a distance rather than 'being' your traumas.

The practice is of course to simply note when your mind begins to follow a thought or a feeling or an awareness of sensation and to gently, without judgment, return your attention to the breath. It doesn't matter if you need to do this many times. The value is in developing the practice of returning to this moment by returning your awareness to this breath.

Spend about two minutes doing this and then pay attention to what happens next; reorienting yourself to the floor below you, the air in the room around you and opening the eyes.

Note: Access a video and audio practice of this at www.TurnAroundTrauma.com.

Although almost everyone can see the value in this exercise, most will discover the real value comes with practice. During this week as you practice this exercise, begin to be aware of and notice when you intuitively practice Mindfulness and mindful awareness of the moment and other situations. For example, if you're stressed in traffic, you might notice when you become aware of the stress that you can automatically focus on your breath rather than letting the stress become a thought you follow. By the end of your first week of practice, you'll notice how natural and easy it is in a variety of different situations and places to mindfully focus on one minute at a time, one moment at a time, one breath at a time.

For the next 21 days, practice this daily, two to three times a day. I can promise, the daily practice will sharpen your axe. It will wire you to the present moment. It will give you a new strategy to stop the wandering mind from becoming anxious about the future or ruminating about the past. It is the practice that activates the potential, not the knowledge of it.

As you advance in your practice, you can add other forms of Mindfulness practice to your routine. One of my favorites is a walking meditation. Each morning I begin my day with a two-mile walk. About 40 minutes. That is a long walk, especially if you are not used to daily walking. I did not begin my day with 2 miles at first. At first, I just walked to the neighborhood park and back. About eight minutes. It's not very far from my house. Then I started walking a little bit further, around the circumference of my neighborhood. It is less than a mile round-trip. After weeks of doing that I slowly expanded my path. I am consistently doing 2 miles every morning now.

I try to make each step a mindful step. Although I am going quite a distance each morning, the distance is the important thing. This is just as effective as if you were to only walk around the block, or up the road and back in ten minutes.

The idea in a walking meditation to is do the same thing as above but instead of paying attention to the breath, you are paying attention to each step. Each step marks each moment, and what you are doing is practicing returning your awareness to the feeling of the sidewalk below your feet, to the weather that surrounds you, to the sensations in your body.

In years gone by when I walked, my mind was swimming. I started to remember everything I was afraid of, and everything I should worry about. Now, because I make each step a connection to this moment, I notice my walks are more productive. I do not become impatient about "getting enough exercise" and I have stopped using my walking time to ruminate about my mistakes.

As you begin this practice, pay attention to anytime your mind wanders and you start following a thought. You do not have to berate yourself and say, "Oh, that was bad, I was following a thought!" Just stop following the thought. Gently and without judgement return your attention to the step. In fact, it is good when you catch yourself following feeling, thoughts or sensations, it means you are getting it. You are noting what the mind is doing and are changing it so that your orientation is in the present moment. That is powerful.

Years ago I was hired by an eating disorder treatment program to facilitate family therapy in the evenings. My shift began at dinner time. All the therapists were required to eat with the patients. The reason? Dinner time on the eating disorder treatment program is group therapy. What did we teach? Mindful eating.

To this day, I am convinced the experience was more valuable to me than my clients. I grew up with poor eating habits. In a house full if nine people, if dinner was good, I had to scoff down my food to get all that I wanted. If dinner was bad, we had to endure our stepfather demanding we eat each last bite, even if it meant sitting at the table, in the dark, staring at our food long past bedtime. Dinner was punishment. Because of my own experiences, I did not enjoy food or eating, I just tried to get it over with. The result? In my adult world, this pattern was the norm. It has taken great practice for me to enjoy my food, slow down while eating, and make the healthy choices that keep me in top shape.

Mindfulness practice changed by brain. It rewired my associations. Long after I was out of the house I had still brought my family to the dinner table. I was haunted by the past and people who were not dining with me. But the patterns were the same. I am sharing this story so that you can see how almost every element of our adverse life experiences shape us, but how mindfulness can change everything from the issues we carry over into our adult world that are big deals, and the traumas that are less unsettling.

This chapter is the most important chapter in this book, because it gives you specific strategies for making significant change. The important thing to remember is that practice makes perfect. It creates a new automatic response. I wish there was a quick way for you to discover the value, but days, weeks, months, and even years of practice will reveal new ways that this practice has been helpful. There are mountains of evidence to support this, and you can discover more at www.TurnAroundTrauma.com.

CHAPTER SEVEN:

Bilateral stimulation

A lot of people ask me about Posttraumatic Stress Disorder (PTSD), and Eye-Movement Desensitization & Reprocessing (EMDR) so I wanted to include some comments and a strategy in this book. There is no doubt certain childhood and adult traumas when left unaddressed may result in PTSD. PTSD is a specific diagnosis in psychiatry, that is characterized by a very specific set of experiences and problems that result from those experiences.

It is important to note two things. First, not all trauma results in a diagnosis of PTSD. The diagnosis can only be made by a licensed medical or mental health practitioner. Second, even if a person does not meet the diagnostic criteria for PTSD, it is likely the adverse life experiences are still underlying many problems, distressing emotions, and difficulties in navigating the tasks of life.

EMDR is a specific modality in the field of psychotherapy. It is an evidenced-based protocol, which means that it is not just a theory but that a body of evidence has shown it to be effective in reducing symptoms associated with PTSD in particular, and symptoms of other psychological distress. EMDR is not a self-help technology. It is a process that a licensed mental health professional uses in therapy.

The simplified explanation of EMDR is based on a principle called bilateral stimulation. We have a left and a right hemisphere of the brain, each responsible for different facets of our experience. By creating any stimuli between the two hemispheres, such as a sound pattern in the left ear and then the right, we are linking or causing the brain stimuli to respond on both sides. The same thing can be done with a ball, passing it from one hand to the other (right-left stimulation). It could also be visual stimulation, like a hypnotherapists pocket watch or an EMDR practitioner using moving light from the left eye to the right.

Bilateral stimulation works to reduce anxiety and other forms of distress. It can also help us connect what is often referred to as the thinking side of the brain with the feeling part of the brain. It does so because of the nervous system does a great job of reorienting itself to new stimuli.

The way this works is based on evolutionary biology. The fight or flight response is activated to protect us. In cavepeople days, a nomad out gathering food might hear a rustle in the field. The nervous system fires up (remember the hypothalamic-pituitary-adrenal axis from the beginning of this book) to quickly determine its source. It is a wild animal or just wind behind them? Once safety is determined, in this case, not a wild animal, the caveperson will return their attention to the task at hand. This is called habituation. Habituation occurs when we cease to respond to a stimulus.

Multiple ongoing traumas cause us to cease to respond. This is why many people describe themselves as "emotionally numb" in the face of trauma. The adverse experiences have occurred so often it has become the new normal. Intellectually, they know something is unacceptable, but the habituation response has created an ability to stand by while either the self or others are at risk.

Sometimes people with multiple adverse experiences feel like they just don't care anymore. They have come to expect nothing good will happen. These are powerful mind-traps and bilateral stimulation is a proven technique for helping a person to break habituation and start feeling alive again. More importantly, it can help break the helplessness so that a person can take action rather than be paralyzed by adversity.

Here are some techniques that you might find helpful when you are in a period of high anxiety, anger, or depression. You might also find these techniques helpful if you find yourself numb, thinking that you should be bothered by something but just can't seem to respond with the appropriate action or feeling.

1. The tennis ball technique. You do not actually have to have a yellow tennis ball. You can use almost

anything, including a coin, a phone, or a pen. Simply take 60 seconds to mindfully pass the object from one had to the other. Gently toss the object from one hand to the other. Spend another minute passing the item back and forth and using an affirmation about the situation as you pass it back and forth. You can do this aloud or simply say it in your own mind. However, I do prefer speaking aloud as it seems to make it "realer," at least for me. A simple affirmation can be structured this way: "Even though I am _____ I am _____." The blanks can be filled in with whatever is appropriate for you. An example: "Even though I am anxious, I am able to create calm and let go of fear by paying attention to this moment."

Or something like this: "Even though this situation is stressful, I am confident and I am calm." The potential affirmations you can use are endless. Another favorite is: "Even though I find this situation difficult, I accept this moment as being exactly as it is, and I release my fears of the future and live in this moment."

Affirmations work. They work when combined with bilateral stimulation because it integrates the intellectual part of the mind with the emotional part, and because our words have power. We act on what we believe, and we believe what we are told. In fact, affirmations are a powerful way to let go of the lies we have believed that others have told us, such as parents who were emotionally abusive, or lovers who have hurt us with their untrue and unkind words.

2. Listen to YouTube. The great thing about the internet, is everything is on it. YouTube has endless hours of music designed for listening (with headphones, because the right-left stereo recording will play in each ear) that have been designed to lower anxiety and help you practice mindfulness with relaxing music in the background.

3. Safe walking. We can simply stimulate the hemispheres of the brain by paying attention to the left and the right when we are walking. This is of course, the right thing to do at a traffic corner. But most of us simply walk looking forward. Practice opening your awareness by scanning left and right. In the context of walking mindfulness meditation, this is highly effective because so often we walk with the head down just looking at only what is in front of us. We can mindfully walk, noticing and observing that which is to the left, and that which is to the right. It not only makes for a more interesting walk, but it helps us to integrate that thinking and feeling part of the mind and break us from the habit of habituation. It will enlighten your path and help you to feel more observant.

CHAPTER EIGHT:

Security and Significance

What are your deepest needs? Many writers have talked about this subject, with some notable writers being William Glasser M.D., who wrote his book Reality Therapy is the early 1970's. At that time he said our greatest need was to love other people and be capable of receiving love in return. I addressed this in a previous chapter, and think it is a profound recognition of our basic needs. Later, in the 1980's Glasser revisited his earlier work and came to a conclusion, our deepest need can be summed up in one word: Belonging.

Also, in the 1960's Transactional Analysis brought the idea of "I'm OK, You're OK." I think this too can be summed up in belonging. Tony Robbins, the self-help guru who has had bestselling books, movies, seminars, and has even consulted with multiple US presidents gave us six human needs:

- Certainty
- Variety and Uncertainty
- Significance

- Love and Connection
- Growth
- Contribution

One of my favorite books was a religious book published by Robert McGee titled, *The Search for Significance*. McGee used two words to describe our greatest needs: Significance and Security. In his book, McGee advocated meeting these needs on a spiritual level through his brand of faith. I think religion can be a pathway to meet our deepest needs, but religion can also be notoriously brutal and harmful. Trite religious slogans do little to bring us either security or significance and dogma can trap us in a state where we feel we have no power.

It is ok to find security and significance apart from religion. If your religion is healthy then embrace it. But if your religious beliefs are creating powerlessness and fear, it is time to evaluate if they are actually contributing to your wellness and to move past them.

As a person with a history of adverse life experiences, security and significance, love and being loved, belonging, growth and contribution do not come naturally. Developing these aspects of living is part of what you have been missing. Your traumas kept you from feeling secure, your adverse experiences took away your certainty and sense of belonging. The things others did to you, and that you might have even done to yourself require forgiveness to create growth. In addiction counseling it is often said that our emotional age is the age at which we started drinking. Growth

Turn Around Trauma

stops, even if alcohol is not our problem, when our deepest needs are unmet.

I think Tony Robbins is onto something. Although his list is similar in spirit to the others, he also points out that we need variety, and uncertainty. What we need is a balance. In response to trauma, many people compensate with rigidity to avoid insecurity. This is the person who puts all their money into a passbook savings account with no interest rather than realizing the financial benefit of compound interest because it is safe. This is the person who stays in a lonely third shift job never wanting to venture into the daytime where there are other people. This is the person who leaves a marriage whenever things are tough because it's the path of least resistance.

If nobody taught you how to meet your deepest needs, try these ideas as a starting point:

1. Develop certainty by being in the moment. The one thing we can always be certain of is right now. This is why mindfulness is so powerful, it keeps us from sliding off the edge and into anxiety by grounding us in the present moment.

   You can create certainty by engaging in rituals, beginning each day with setting intentions. The foundation of harnessing the power of 'Now' and creating lasting transformation is intention. Nothing that exists in this world exists without intention. A desk does not make itself, a car does not build itself, and even an autonomous vehicle had to be programmed by someone with intention. Intention is what creates our reality and it is for this reason that it is the foundation of certainty. Act with intention and you are acting in the moment.

2. Create spontaneity and uncertainty. In the past you did this by stirring up chaos. Now, you are going to do this by finding that which is fascinating in the tasks of life. By observing the breath, we are discovering this moment, it makes life interesting and living more powerful.

3. Use affirmations to boost your significance. Affirmations are not pie in the sky hopes and wishes, powerful affirmations are those things which boost our significance when we hear the truth. Right now, identify three things that are right with you. The temptation is of course, to start thinking about all the deficiencies. Forget about them. What is right with you? I know it's a hard question but it's essential you come up with three. Write them down, right here in the book (it's okay to write in a book):

One:

Two:

Three:

Now take a dry erase marker and write these things on the bathroom mirror. It will be a powerful way to both start and end the day, since the bathroom mirror is often both the first and the last thing we see in the day.

4. Let yourself love. Give yourself permission to love, to take risks and to share with others. I am not talking here about romantic love, although you can be open in this area if you are strong enough at this time. What I am talking about is simply practicing compassion for others because they too are a person with value and worth. When you practice compassion you are practicing love. Start by forgiving other drivers. Let them in when they are turning left in a busy place. Start by taking in a breath and being in the moment when the clerk at a store is rude and tired. Worry about yourself and start having compassion and patience with others. After all, we do not know what their adverse life experiences are.

5. Read another book. I am glad you have read this book, almost to the end. Learning creates growth. Seek out opportunities to grow and grow with other people. Avoid isolation and find like-minded people in anything ranging from a positive support group to a hobbyist group.

6. Find your contribution. Each one of us can find ways to contribute to a better world. Sometimes it can be as simple as picking up the trash other people leave behind, and other times it means getting involved with non-profits as a volunteer or serving others by sharing our experiences.

Find ways you can contribute to a better world. It will make you a better person.

CHAPTER NINE:

Getting Additional Help

Sigmund Freud pioneered the first approach to contemporary psychology. His approach in a simplistic term, was that we need to talk about the past. What Freud got correct was that our past impacts us. What he got wrong was the need to talk about it. The need is to live in the present, no matter what the past.

Contemporary psychotherapy still often begins with the past. Therapists want us to tell our story, so they can also discover where we come from. But therapy should focus on the present, and not retraumatize us. We cannot change the past. No matter how we revisit it, it cannot be undone. The only moment we can impact is this present moment.

One of Freud's central ideas was that we could go back into the past to find the cause of today's issue. He thought we could resolve that past problem through a series of different processes and then experience life more fully in the present. It made for a great theory in the early 1900s, but the evidence shows us that we can't impact the past at all. In fact, the evidence shows us that memory isn't particularly accurate or even useful in many cases; as a result, regression to a specific cause and resolving that cause is an ineffective method as contrasted with those approaches of Mindfulness based therapies.

One of the most amazing effects of using Mindfulness following trauma is how we figuratively change the past by changing the present. It's not because the past is altered or because it's even resolved, or because somehow the past is different. Rather, through the processes of acceptance, we can change either the importance of the past or our interpretation of the past. The result is that we are no longer enmeshed with the troubling past, instead enjoying this present moment to its maximum potential.

This book has been a collection of ideas that can help you move forward by seizing the power of this moment. It is not a substitute for professional help. Professional counseling can be a support that can help you with this endeavor. Here are some guidelines to help you determine if this is a direction that would benefit you:

Many people do benefit from professional counseling. It can be a life-changing experience. Professional counseling teaches people to take control over their own life and to manage difficult emotions when those emotions are getting in the way of having successful relationships.

Here are some examples of when you would benefit

by finding a professional to support you and help you:

1. When you are self-sabotaging your health, your relationships, and your work.
2. When you wish revenge or harm to other people.
3. When you are unable to communicate with others without it escalating into larger problems.
4. When your own depressions, anxiety, or anger is impacting your health and wellness.
5. When you feel guilt for making the right decisions.
6. When you feel alone, isolated, and without support.
7. When it seems nothing you have done has helped the situations that are distressing.
8. When you look for escape in unhealthy outlets such as gambling, sex, drugs, shopping or other high-risk areas that can cause you additional problems.
9. When others stop listening to you and you feel all bridges have been burned.
10. When you do not feel safe.

Seeking professional help is not a sign of weakness, it is a sign of strength. Therapists have the right training, the right experience and the right skills to help you with almost any situation. They will help you uncover new options, learn communications strategies and manage your emotions.

There are many different types of therapists. It is important to know what you are looking for. My suggestion, when dealing with the dynamic's adverse childhood experiences, is to seek out a Licensed Marriage and Family Therapist. The American Association for Marriage and Family Therapy has a directory, and a link can be found on the www.TurnAroundTrauma.com website.

Psychiatrists are medical doctors who treat mental illness, often with medication and frequently without counseling. They usually refer patients to counselors for psychotherapy in addition to medication management. They are not generally the first contact for therapy and counseling. I would suggest looking for an AAMFT marriage and family therapist first, they will refer you to a psychiatrist if necessary.

Psychologists may often specialize in trauma recovery work, but this profession is very diverse so if you choose to see a psychologist, ask if they have specialized training in the approaches of mindfulness-based therapies.

Licensed Professional Counselors (also called Licensed Mental Health Counselors in some states) are another resource, especially for individual counseling. Most have training in contemporary approaches to helping people with adverse life experiences.

Social workers in private practice may also focus on marriage and family therapy issues. The field of social work is very broad but private practitioners doing psychotherapy with clients are often skilled in these issues as well.

The qualifications for any of these professions include

advanced degrees, clinical supervision and state licensure. By seeing a licensed member of any of these professions you can be certain they have the training and expertise to assist you.

Before you make any appointment, spend a few minutes interviewing a potential therapist. Ask about their qualifications and experience in these areas. Any professional should be open to a brief interview, and if you cannot get this move along to another professional to make sure you will "fit" before booking a session.

Health insurance will often pay for some of the costs associated with marriage and family therapy, subject to your deductibles, co-pays and policy limits. Some therapists work on a sliding-scale to decrease the out of pocket expense.

CHAPTER TEN:

Oogway's gift

Master Oogway gave us a gift. His profound explanation of the value of the present moment. As I conclude this book my hope is that you will accept his gift, and that you will benefit from the simple techniques offered to help you make the value of mindfulness real. I have. The many clients I have worked with have. Millions of other people who have been inspired by TEDx talks on mindfulness, or learned mindfulness in other ways, also testify to the present being a gift.

This book is titled *Turn Around Trauma* because trauma and adversity set us on one course, but at any time we have an ability to see a different side. We don't have to overcome, overpower, or get rid of our trauma. We just need to turn it around and find a new vantage point. This moment provides a safe vantagepoint.

We can change the angle of our perception and put some space between us and our pain by practicing the principles of mindfulness, cognitive defusion, bilateral stimulation, distancing, resilience, and acceptance.

These principles are all embodied in the simple words of Master Oogway.

Another word of wisdom from the cartoon turtle Oogway is, "Your mind is like this water, my friend. When it gets agitated, it becomes difficult to see. But if you allow it to settle, the answer becomes clear." This book has given you the starting point for letting the mind settle. The results of the practices in this book will provide clarity. Trauma and adversity clouds the water of life. It does so by training us to believe our anxiety and fear is a way to problem solve, that our anger is a source of energy, and that our depression is valuable. When the cloudy water settles and you put some space between you and your adversity, it is always clearer.

If you have read this book to the end, you have hope. Contrary to the popular cliché "Hope is not a strategy", hope is a strategy! Hope drives change. You have a starting point, the exercises in this book, and you can graduate from the strategies here to a daily practice of mindfulness and realize even more power in the moment. You can do this with self-study, there are resources on the TurnAroundTrauma.com website to help you with that, and there are peer supports you can discover, along with professional counseling resources that are available to you.

For some reading this book it will at first appear overwhelming to step into hope and live in the moment. Again, Oogway offered us more profound words, "If you only do what you can do, you will never be more than you are now." How do you do more than you can do?

Learn more and practice. This book has been a starting point. Turning around trauma is about breaking the patterns of first response and doing something entirely different. It took years of adversity and years of trauma to bring you to a point where you sought solutions, and so continue to seek and continue to practice. The results will be powerful.

Hope is real! It's interesting that so any people seem to question if hope is real, but nobody ever seems to question if hopelessness is real. By mindfully being in this moment you are setting aside the reality of hopelessness, and literally breathing in hope. You do not have to try to be hopeful, just be hopeful, accept it, don't wonder if its lasting, just be filled with hope in this moment. Open the gift from our cartoon friend and enjoy the moment. After all, you survived this long, you might as well bask in the joy of this moment right now because right now, no matter where you have been in life, you have arrived in a very special place: this moment.

Please visit:

TurnAroundTrauma.com

to access the additional resources the author has provided for your benefit.

You can access Dr. Nongard's TEDx talk, and a collection of other resources, on this website. You can also discover how to purchase additional books by Dr. Nongard, and how you can bring him as a motivational speaker to your community or professional group.

Printed in Great Britain
by Amazon